Ephesians—The Epistle of Christian Maturity

*This is a self-study course
designed to help you discover
for yourself, from the Bible,
some important basic truths about
living the Christian life.*

how to study the lesson

1. Try to find a quiet spot free from distractions and noise.

2. Read the entire Scripture lesson; read it several times to help you absorb its content.

3. Read each question carefully. Then look up the Scripture reference given after each question. Make sure you have found the correct Scripture passage. For example, sometimes you may find yourself looking up JOHN 1:1 instead of I JOHN 1:1.

4. Answer the question from the appropriate Bible passage. Write, in your own words, a phrase or sentence to answer the question. In questions that can be answered with a "yes" or "no" always give the reason for your answer . . . "Yes, because. . . ."

5. If possible, keep a dictionary handy in order to look up words you don't understand.

1

6. Pray for God's help. You *need* God's help in order to understand what you study in the Bible. Psalm 119:18 would be an appropriate verse for you to take to God in prayer.

7. *Class teachers using this course for group study will find some helpful suggestions on page 63.*

how to
take the self-check tests

Each lesson is concluded with a test designed to help you evaluate what you have learned.

1. Review the lesson carefully in the light of the self-check test questions.

2. If there are any questions in the self-check test you cannot answer, perhaps you have written into your lesson the wrong answer from your Bible. Go over your work carefully to make sure you have filled in the blanks correctly.

3. When you think you are ready to take the self-check test, do so without looking up the answers.

4. Check your answers to the self-check test carefully with the answer key given on page 48.

5. If you have any questions wrong, your answer key will tell you where to find the correct answer in your lesson. Go back and locate the right answers. Learn by your mistakes!

apply
what you have learned
to your own life

In this connection, read carefully JAMES 1:22-25. It is only as you apply your lessons to your own life that you will really grow in grace and increase in the knowledge of God.

Introduction to Ephesians

Coleridge called the epistle to the Ephesians "the divinest composition of man." It was written by the apostle Paul about A.D. 62. He had been a prisoner at Rome at least a year. Paul's remarkable labors at Ephesus are recorded in ACTS 18 and 19.

The subject of the epistle is the believer's place in Christ and Christ's place in the believer. God's highest thought for His Church will be found in this letter.

If you try to read a letter that was written to someone else, sometimes it will make very little sense. If you are one of those to whom this epistle was written, it will mean much to you, otherwise you will need to accept Christ as Saviour before you can fully comprehend it.

The epistle is divided into two parts: (1) Doctrinal—chapters 1-3, and (2) Practical—chapters 4-6. The key statement for the first section is, "That ye may know what is the hope of his calling" (1:18). The key statement for the second section is, "That ye walk worthy of the vocation wherewith ye are called" (4:1).

Outline of the Book

The Mystery
of the Church

1:1-14

1. To whom is this letter addressed?

1:1 _The Saints and Faithful in Jesus Christ_

2. According to the wonderful doxology of verse 3, what has been given to every true Christian?

1:3 _Spiritual Blessings in Heavenly Places_

3. As Christians, what do we need to know most of all?

I CORINTHIANS 2:12 _God Loves us and will take Care of us_

4. From what can all our needs be supplied?

PHILIPPIANS 4:19 _The riches and Glory in Christ Jesus_

5. How are all spiritual blessings to be found?

1:3; compare COLOSSIANS 2:10 _Spiritual Blessings Come through Christ Jesus_

The expression "heavenly places" is found five times in Ephesians, so that some refer to this epistle as "the Alps of the New Testament." This is quite in contrast with the book of Ecclesiastes in the Old Testament, the key phrase of which is "under the sun." Paul takes us to the heights for our spiritual outlook.

The "spiritual blessings" are now enumerated in verses 4-14 and they are threefold:

Verses 4-6 *Predestinated*—grace originating in the Father's love before the foundation of the world.

Verses 7-12 *Purchased*—grace wrought out by the suffering of the Son.

Verses 13, 14 *Preserved*—grace confirmed by the operation of the Holy Spirit.

Note how each section ends with praise to God, His grace and His glory.

A divine plan of salvation

6. Why have we been chosen in Christ?

1:4 *We should be holy without . blame*

7. How far back does this plan of perfecting a peculiar people unto Himself go?

1:4 *Befor the World was made.*

8. What else is said to have been before the foundation of the world?

JOHN 1:1, 2 *The Word*

9. What else was foreordained before the world?

I PETER 1:19, 20 *Sheding of Blood of Chrust*

10. What does John tell us about the pre-existence of the divine Son?

JOHN 1:2 *He was With God in beginning (before the World)*

11. How were true believers seen in the purpose of God before the worlds were made?

II TIMOTHY 1:9 *God*

12. Unto what are believers predestinated ("checked off beforehand")?

1:5 _Adoption of Sons_

13. What else was included in God's predestination?

ROMANS 8:29 _Image of Christ_

14. What comes ahead of God's predestination of believers?

ROMANS 8:29; I PETER 1:2 _____

_____

As someone puts it: Outside heaven's gate we may read: "Whosoever *will* may enter." But when you get inside, you may read on the other side of the gate: "Whosoever *would* was foreknown and checked off in the eternal councils." Bear in mind there is no word to the unsaved about predestination. The gospel is for *whosoever*.

15. When one is marked off beforehand, what makes him acceptable to God?

1:6 _He hath made us through his grace_

16. How do we become children of God?

JOHN 3:7; compare EPHESIANS 1:5 _TO ACCEPT SALVATION_

Note that there are two aspects of sonship: (1) *Generative*—through a heavenly birth we partake of the divine nature. (2) *Adoption*—the word for "adoption" means "son-placing," suggesting a *legal* transaction into the full privileges of the family. That is, a Christian is immediately placed in the position of a full grown son, which makes him a full heir; a "joint heir with Jesus Christ"—the Son from eternity.

17. What is the price that gives us entrance to heaven?

1:7 _JESUS BLOOD_

18. What does the believer experience when he is saved?

1:7 _FORGIVNESS OF OUR TRESPASSES_
RICHES OF HIS GRACE

19. "Redemption" means a price paid to deliver one from what?

I THESSALONIANS 1:10 _THE WRATH TO COME_

20. What attributes of God are illuminated by His grace?

1:8 _WISDOM & INSIGHT_
Prudence

A divine mystery revealed

21. The divine plan of redemption looks forward to what occasion?

1:10 _THE SUMMING UP OF ALL THINGS IN_
CHRIST

The word for "dispensation" means "a stewardship." The Greek word forms the basis for our English word "economy." The same word is used in LUKE 16:2-4: "Give account of thy stewardship"—administration, house management. All points toward "the stewardship of the fullness of times" when Christ is coming to be "glorified in his saints" (II THESSALONIANS 1:10). Then He will "gather together in one" —literally, "head up for Himself in one"—the whole universe. Jesus the true Steward will, in the fullness of seasons, come and take possession of all His inheritance.

A divine inheritance

22. How should the knowledge of such an inheritance cause us to live?

1:12 _PRAISE GOD FOR HIS GLORY_

23. How is this inheritance described?

I Peter 1:4 _INPTERSHIBLE, UNO EFICABLE, CAN NOT BE TAKEN AWAY_

We read now concerning the inheritor's *guarantee*. This doctrine applies only to those genuinely born of the Spirit, raised in Christ to newness of life.

24. What happens when one really hears the gospel and believes it?

1:13 _SEALED IN WITH THE HOLY SPIRUT_

The words "after that" in both instances in this verse should read "when." This sealing takes place at the time of salvation. It is the stamp of God upon a life that designates it as God's property.

25. What one thing is necessary in our salvation?

I Peter 1:23-25; James 1:18 _THE WORD OF GOD Being Born Again_

A *seal* suggests three things:

1. Ownership. Entrance of the Holy Spirit into the life through the new birth marks one as belonging to God. It is a legal act of God, not an emotional experience.

2. A seal is used to prevent molestation—of letters, documents, packages (Matthew 27:63-65). The believer is guaranteed unto the end (I Corinthians 1:8).

3. A seal is a mark of acceptance. The Jewish priest examined the sacrificial lamb and if there was no defect, he put the temple seal upon it as fit for sacrifice. Of Jesus we read: "Him hath God the Father sealed" (John 6:27). He was the Lamb without blemish.

26. The Holy Spirit is what part of our inheritance?

1:14 _a pledge to Gods own inheritance_

The word for "earnest" means the "first installment." The Holy Spirit is the pledge of our salvation until it is completely consummated at Christ's coming.

27. How far does this "until" stretch? *Or we get to heaven*

EPHESIANS 4:30 *Until Day of Redemption to collect*

28. What does this future redemption include?

ROMANS 8:23 *Redemption of our Bodies*

29. Of what will those who carry the seal of that future day be certain?

I PETER 1:4, 5 *An Inheritance undefiled cared for By God and prepared By God*

Note that the seal marks God's claim on us. The earnest of the Spirit is our claim on God. Have you received eternal life?

Yes

30. Of what one thing can we be confident (rely on)?

PHILIPPIANS 1:6 *That if we obey God and follow Him He will perfect it until Christ comes for us*

check-up time No. 1

You have just studied some important truths about the mystery of the Church. Review your study by rereading the questions and your written answers. If you are not sure of an answer, reread the Scripture portion given to find the answer. Then take this test to see how well you understand important truths you have studied.

In the right-hand margin write "True" or "False" after each of the following statements.

1. Christians' blessings are of a material nature.

2. Christians are chosen in Christ before the foundation of the world.

3. The Christian is expected to live a holy life.

4. Divine predestination is linked with divine fore-knowledge.

5. Man can be saved by his own good works.

6. Since our inheritance is assured, we may live as we please.

7. The Holy Spirit seals believers in Christ, marking them out as belonging to God.

8. Our entire inheritance as believers is reserved for us in glory.

9. The resurrection of the believer's body is included in the plan of redemption.

10. Eventually all things are to be gathered together in Christ.

Turn to page 64 and check your answers.

A Prayer for the Church

1:15-23

1. In what way did Paul continue to remember the saints at Ephesus?

1:16 _In Prayer_

2. Name several of the things Paul requested for the Christians.

1:17 _a Spirit of wisdom AND of revelation IN THE Knowledge of Him_

3. What was the first thing that Paul prayed the saints might come to discern? _Wisdom / Knowledge of God_

1:17 _THAT CHrist may Dwell IN your Hearts THrough faith_

4. What is the hope of God's calling? _SALVATION_

1:18; ROMANS 8:29 _THaT we may Know The riches of The glory of THE Inheritance IN THE SAINTS, For ALL THINGS work Together For good For THOSE CALLED ACCORDING To His_

5. List the second thing Paul wanted us to understand. _purpose_

1:18 _So THAT we may Know THE riches of THE glory AND Inheritance accorDing To our works for our purpose Here_

6. What does the Lord count as His precious inheritance?

DEUTERONOMY 32:9 _His people_

12

7. For this reason, what was the prayer of Christ?

JOHN 17:24 _Christ prayed we would be with him_

8. Who are the most highly blessed people on earth?

PSALM 33:12 _Christians People of the nation who God is the Lord Because He has Chosen us for His own_

9. What is the special privilege of those who are God's inheritance?

JEREMIAH 15:16 _God calls us By name_

10. List the third thing Paul desired for converts.

1:19 _That God would Surpass His greatness and Power to us who Believe So That we might work according to The Power of His might_

Power through Jesus Christ

11. What had been accomplished by this same "power"?

1:20 _God raised Christ from The Dead And Seated Him on The right in Heaven_

Here is the security for our covenant. The forces of corruption are mighty, the adversary powerful, but He who reigns for us and dwells within us is *mightier*.

12. How great is the name of the One who lives to empower us?

1:21 _God is far above all rule & Authority Power + Dominion And Every name That is named_

The words "every name that is named" are more literally, "everything that can bear a name." It takes in more than persons; *anything* or *anyone* you mention—Christ is greater.

13. What is the relation of the true Church to Him who has supreme dominion over every thing, every creature and "all power in heaven and in earth"?

1:22 _All things are in subjection under his feet, He is head over all things to the Church_

14. Record also the statement made as to the place of the Church in relation to Him.

1:23 _Which in his body the fulness of Him who fills all in all_

The word "fullness" in verse 23 literally means "completeness."

15. If this is the case, of what are true believers assured?

JOHN 6:37 _That if you come to Him He will not cast you out_

Without Eve, we are told that Adam was incomplete. She was of his body and when united to him she was declared one spirit, bone and flesh with him. Without Christ the universe would be incomplete; without His true Church, Christ would be incomplete. She is the "completeness of Him who filleth all with the elements and entities of which they are composed."

check-up time No. 2

You have just studied some important truths about prayer and power in the early church. Now take this test to see how well you understand important truths you have studied.

Circle the letter of the correct or most nearly correct answer.

1. Paul continually remembered the Ephesians in (a) prayer, (b) private conversation, (c) greetings to other churches.

2. Paul prayed that the Ephesians might have more (a) wealth, (b) wisdom, (c) willingness.

3. God's inheritance is (a) shared with the angels, (b) in heaven, (c) in the saints.

4. The power of God is described in Ephesians as (a) excellent, (b) dynamic, (c) mighty.

5. God's power has been demonstrated particularly in (a) raising Christ from the dead, (b) creating the universe, (3) preserving the saints.

6. Christ is now seated (a) in the heavenly temple, (b) on the throne of David, (c) in heavenly places.

7. Christ's exaltation is above (a) principality and power, (b) might and dominion, (c) all of these.

8. In Ephesians, Christ is described as (a) the Lamb, (b) the Lion, (c) Head of the Church.

9. The Church is described as (a) Christ's bride, (b) Christ's fullness, (c) the army of heaven.

10. Christ's name is (a) the greatest of all, (b) superior to Gabriel's, (c) not mentioned in Ephesians.

Turn to page 64 and check your answers.

15

The Creation of the Church

2:1-22

In the book of Romans the moral corruption of the whole world is demonstrated: the Gentile without the law and the Jew with his law are equally guilty and lost.

Ephesians is addressed to the individual after he is saved. Chapter 2 shows the material out of which he was made before the grace of God took hold of him.

1. How is it possible for one to be dead and very much alive physically at the same time?

2:1; ROMANS 8:6 _Dead Spiritually Alive Only Physically_

2. What is true of some people who think they are enjoying life?

I TIMOTHY 5:6 _They are Dead Spiritualy even while Living_

3. What was told to one who had high moral standards but was insensible to the Spirit of God?

JOHN 3:3 _Unless you are Born Again you many not See the Kingdom of god_

4. When one is spiritually dead, to what spirit is his mind most susceptible?

2:2 _Satan God of this world_

5. Since Satan is the spiritual father of some people, whose will are they prone to obey?

JOHN 8:44 _Their Father Satan_

6. Although some may have high intellectual and moral standards, to what great class do they belong if they are rejecting Christ?

2:2 _The world Satan sons of Disobedience_

7. Since they do not have the new nature, what nature do they have?

2:3 _Natures of Their own Flesh_

8. By what are their lives predominantly controlled?

2:3 _Desires of The Flesh and of The mind_

9. What does it mean to be a child of wrath?

2:3; compare JOHN 3:36 _You Are no different from the Unsaved if you give into Desires of The_
When man is at the end of himself, then—"but *God*" (1:4).   _flesh_

Salvation through grace

10. List three things that may become the experience of true believers through the mercy and love of God.

a. 2:5 _All By Grace Are Saved Even Though all were Dead By our own Transgreitions_

b. 2:6 _if saved will All Be with Him in Heaven_

c. 2:6 _And raised up_

11. To what must this experience be attributed?

2:5 _Salvation (made us Alive Together)_

12. Who is said to be seated in heavenly places?

1:20 _Christ At Gods Right Hand_

13. As to position, what place does every Son of God occupy?

2:6 _Seated us with Him_

17

14. If we are indeed risen in Christ, what should we seek?

COLOSSIANS 3:1, 2 _____

15. Where is the believer's true life?

COLOSSIANS 3:3 _____

The "quickening" imparts life. The raising has to do with the placing of that life in its proper sphere in Christ. Seated in heavenly places in Christ means that we are perfectly secure. Our complete identification with the Christ of glory guarantees this.

16. As we look into past ages, what do we see was planned before the foundation of the world?

1:4 _He has chosen us in him_

17. As we look into the future eternity, what do we learn as to why God saved us?

2:7 _To show us his exceeding riches of his grace and kindness_

18. When is God's perfected work in His saints first to be displayed for the admiration of all?

II THESSALONIANS 1:10 _When he shall come to be glorified_

19. What is God going to do during the Kingdom Age?

1:10 _He will gather together in one all things in Christ_

20. How long will God display before the universe what He accomplished through the gift of His Son?

2:7 _That in ages to come (forever)_

21. How long will the redeemed be giving glory to God?

3:21 _Through all ages)_

18

22. To what intent is this eternal display of the wonders of grace?

3:10 _So the Church will know of God's wisdom_

The superficial thinker might take this as a doctrine of almighty selfishness—the self-pleasure of God. But the spiritually minded will apprehend God's plan, an eternal reminder to the saved of what might have been but for God's grace in Christ—a display to all heavenly beings of the product of Christ's redemption.

The apostle now comes back to remind us of the present operations of grace through contact with Jesus Christ.

23. Of what do we constantly need to be reminded regarding our salvation?

2:9, 10 _____

The construction of the Greek makes the last phrase of verse 8 refer to the whole verse, so that we cannot even boast of our faith. Even in that we have the assistance of the Holy Spirit (see JOHN 6:44; HEBREWS 12:1, 2; PHILIPPIANS 1:29). Spurgeon once said: "Don't make the mistake of making a christ out of your faith, as if it was an independent source of salvation."

24. While we have no works that we can offer God toward our salvation, what is the ultimate purpose of salvation which comes through the new birth?

2:10 _____

25. What is the only way we can appropriately boast?

PSALM 34:2 _____

26. What will come out of those who have the divine Worker within them?

TITUS 3:5, 8 _____

_____

The Greek word translated "workmanship" in EPHESIANS 2:10 is *poiema*, which means "poem." A poem is a composition into which deep thoughts are compressed in few words. Every believer is the special creation of the mind of God and He has a plan for each life which, if sought and followed, will demonstrate the concentrated wisdom of God.

A picture of the unbeliever

27. List the five things that are said about the unregenerate.

2:12 _____

_____

_____

28. What was the true "commonwealth" of Israel?

ROMANS 2:28, 29 _____.

29. Describe the state of nearly all Gentiles, as well as those who boasted of being Israelites.

ROMANS 1:21 _____

_____

30. *But now*—after Israel also had rejected the Saviour—what new and living way had been opened for all who would receive it?

2:13 _____

31. State the one basis of finding peace.

2:14 _____

32. When do we have peace with God through Jesus Christ?

ROMANS 5:1 _____

Note that Christ Himself is our peace. He is more than simply a peacemaker. In His person as the God-man He is our peace just as He is our Saviour (ACTS 4:12).

33. What has been broken down as a result of Christ's redemptive work?

2:14 _____

34. Describe Israel's position of separation from the nations prior to that time.

ISAIAH 5:1, 2; MATTHEW 21:33 _____

_____

In Herod's temple there was a dividing wall five feet high to separate Gentiles who came into the temple from the Jews. This was the cause of much hostile feeling against the Jews. Note the Jews' charge against Paul in ACTS 21:28. At the cross of Calvary the ground is level. "We are all one in Christ Jesus."

35. What "abolished" (literally "rendered idle") the laws and ordinances that separated Jews and Gentiles?

2:15; COLOSSIANS 1:21, 22 _____

_____

36. What happened to these separating ordinances?

COLOSSIANS 2:14 _____

37. For whom is Christ the end of the law for righteousness?

ROMANS 10:4 _____

38. The cross has what effect upon believing Jew and Gentile?

2:16 _____

The Slain One slays the slayer, sin, by His death on the cross, the instrument on which He Himself was slain. Apart from what took place at Calvary, no such bond between Jew and Gentile is possible.

39. To what two classes is Christ's peace offered?

2:17 _____

40. What is the sole road to reconciliation with God?

COLOSSIANS 1:20, 21 _____

41. Name the three Infinite Persons who are linked in the working out of this salvation for us.

2:18 _____

The Church a spiritual body

42. State the position now of believing Jew and Gentile.

2:19 _____

43. In what kingdom do these saints now hold citizenship?

COLOSSIANS 1:13 _____

44. To what kind of "nation" do all saints belong?

I PETER 2:9 _____

The word for "household" in verse 19 literally means "kinsfolk." The same word is found in I TIMOTHY 5:8 stressing the duty of providing for kinsfolk.

45. What figure does the apostle now use to set forth another aspect of our relationship in Christ?

2:20-22 _____

46. What needs to be thoroughly understood about the foundation?

2:20; compare I CORINTHIANS 3:11 _____

_____

47. To what does Peter compare every true believer?

I PETER 2:4, 5 _____

48. What is the purpose of the cementing together of true believers by the Holy Spirit?

2:22 _____

The Church of Christ is not composed merely of all churches, or the sum total of church members. It consists of all people genuinely born from above, cemented by the Holy Spirit to the one Foundation. It is no mere self-help society or social betterment organization. It is a spiritual structure in which the power of God is manifested in the world.

check-up time No. 3

You have just studied some important truths about the creation of the Church. Review your study by rereading the questions and your written answers. If you are not sure of an answer, reread the Scripture portion given to find the answer. Then take this test to see how well you understand important truths you have studied.

In the right-hand margin write "True" or "False" after each of the following statements.

1. Unbelievers are actually spiritually dead. _____

2. There is an evil spirit who influences those who disobey the gospel. _____

3. Unsaved people are usually controlled by high and pure motives. _____

4. Conversion is a very real experience. _____

5. Salvation is by sincerity and good works. _____

6. The redeemed are going to be an endless source of glory to God. _____

7. Those who are truly saved reveal it by doing good works. _____

8. Jews have a better chance of salvation than Gentiles. _____

9. The difference between Jew and Gentile is abolished in Christ. _____

10. The apostle uses the figure of a building to describe the true Church. _____

Turn to page 64 and check your answers.

The Heavenly Calling of the Church

3:1-21

1. With what three words does this chapter open?

3:1 _____

These words point to the closing words of the previous chapter (2:20-22).

2. What is the great construction project of which Paul is thinking as he carries on the argument in chapter 3?

2:20-22 _____

3. To what special mission was Paul appointed in connection with the materials of the great spiritual temple?

3:8, 9 _____

4. How did the apostle describe this special commission?

ACTS 22:21 _____

_____

5. How did the Jews react to the idea of Paul's preaching salvation to the Gentiles?

ACTS 22:22 _____

6. In connection with this commission, what was made known to Paul?

3:2-5 _____

This "mystery" is referred to six times in Ephesians.

7. How does Paul refer to his commission?

3:2 _____.

On the word "dispensation" refer back to 1:10. It means "management of a household" or "stewardship." Through the grace of God a special stewardship was assigned to Paul, giving him great responsibility toward the Gentiles.

8. How long had this secret of one spiritual body of both Jewish and Gentile believers been held back?

ROMANS 16:25 _____

The words "since the world began" in ROMANS 16:25 are more literally translated, "during the periods of ages." We have already seen that the Church was in the counsels of God before the foundation of a world, but God let ages go by until He was ready to make known the deeper meaning of the promise given Abraham. This had reference to an earthly seed, compared to the "sands of the sea," and a spiritual seed, compared to "the stars of heaven." It was now openly revealed —a body of believing Jews and Gentiles, united by the Holy Spirit to the risen Christ. In the special interests of this project, Paul was appointed.

A revelation of the mystery

9. How did Paul come to understand this mystery?
3:3; compare ROMANS 16:25; EPHESIANS 1:9, 10 _____

_____

10. Who also shared in the knowledge of this mystery?

3:5 _____

11. Was this "mystery" made known in Old Testament times?

COLOSSIANS 1:25 _____

12. To whom was this mystery now made manifest?

COLOSSIANS 1:26 _____

13. When did Christ assume headship of His Body, the true Church?

1:20-23 _____

14. When did the Holy Spirit first baptize believers into one body?

I CORINTHIANS 12:13; compare ACTS 2:2-4 _____

_____

15. Who were included in that body formed at Pentecost?

ACTS 2:39; compare EPHESIANS 2:13 _____

_____

16. Who had previously indicated by His teachings that the gospel was not to be confined to Jewry?

MATTHEW 13:38 _____

17. When the Saviour gave His Great Commission, to whom did He open the doors of His Church?

MATTHEW 28:19; ACTS 1:8 _____

_____

18. Who was first prepared for the great truth that the Body of Christ was to be comprised of some from all nations?

ACTS 15:7-11 _____

19. Upon whom was the Church of this age built?

Ephesians 2:20 _____

20. How is the "mystery" now defined?

3:6 _____

_____

Note that it is not simply that Gentiles can now be saved. Those who had a desire for truth in the Old Testament period could be saved. Also the Old Testament abounds in promises to the Gentile nations in the Kingdom Age. But there is no hint of being joint heirs with Israel, fellow members of the same body through the Holy Spirit.

21. What removed the "partition" between Jew and Gentile and put all on the same basis for salvation?

2:13, 14 _____

Respond to the calling

22. What was the marvel to Paul that he should be called to preach to the Gentiles?

3:8 _____

23. What else did Paul call himself?

I Timothy 1:15 _____

24. How do these expressions reveal a great work of grace in Paul's heart?

Philippians 3:5; Galatians 1:13, 14 _____

_____

25. What was God's purpose in the mystery?

3:10 _____

26. What "principalities in heavenly places" might be meant?

6:12; I Peter 1:10-12 _____

_____

27. What is the effect upon angels when people are saved?

Luke 15:7 _____

28. In what class of beings are angels now interested?

Hebrews 1:14 _____

Think of it, the true Church, to which you belong if you are born again, is the highest revelation of the manifold wisdom of God, even to angels.

29. Where is the family of God now located geographically?

3:15 _____

Unlimited resources

30. State Paul's first petition for the Christian.

3:16 _____

_____

In verse 16, the Greek word for "might" is *dunamis* (power for enablement). The words for "inner man" may be rendered "deep in you."

31. What is the next petition?

3:17a _____

The word for "dwell" means "make His home with"—permanent dweller.

32. What two things did Paul desire in regard to the Christian's love?

3:17 _____

_____

"Rooted"—like a tree sending down its roots into the soil of divine love (ROMANS 5:5; GALATIANS 5:22). "Grounded"—like a building with its foundation laid on divine love.

33. What is the next petition?

3:18 _____

Note that verse 18 does not specifically state to what these four dimensions apply. Some try to take them as referring to the love of God in verse 19, but observe that verse 19 begins with "and," which separates thoughts in Greek construction. Furthermore, that which is mentioned in verse 19 "passes knowledge," whereas the prayer of verse 18 is that we may be able to comprehend. Verse 18 has to do with something that the apostle wishes us to contemplate in its measurements, but the infinite love of God is boundless. It is incapable of any full comprehension.

34. What is the great subject so prominent as to make its repetition unnecessary?

2:21, 22; compare 3:1, 14, 17 _____

_____

35. What was being built as a monument of grace to principalities and powers in heavenly places for all eternity?

3:10 _____

36. What had once been the subject of comment by some of the disciples?

MARK 13:1, 2 _____

37. To what other structure did Peter refer later?

I Peter 2:4, 5 _____

38. What did Jesus say about this same structure?

Matthew 16:18 _____

Paul now prays that Christians may have some concept of the greatness of this spiritual house, the depth of the Rock on which it is founded, the height of its cornice and the various kinds of stones that are in it. Our task as Christians is to help add "living stones," until it is ready for the capstone which, of course, is Christ.

39. Concerning what does the apostle now pray that we might have an "experiential knowledge," even though the thing itself passes comprehension?

3:19 _____

40. State the last petition in your own words.

3:19b _____

_____

The last is literally, "that ye may have poured into you the all-embracing ocean of God's plentitude." Is it asking too much to allow Him to fill us to capacity? The ocean is not too great to hold His glory and the dewdrop is not too small.

check-up time No. 4

You have just studied some important truths about the calling of the Church. Now take this test to see how well you understand important truths you have studied.

Circle the letter of the correct or most nearly correct answer.

1. The opening words of Ephesians chapter 2 (a) link on to what has already been said, (b) are not in the original, (c) should be omitted.

2. The "mystery" was made known (a) to Paul only, (b) to the Jews, (c) to Paul and others.

3. Believers were first baptized into the body of Christ (a) when Christ arose from the dead, (b) on the day of Pentecost, (c) at Christ's ascension.

4. The Lord told the disciples that they were to (a) preach only to Jews, (b) preach only to Gentiles, (c) preach to all men.

5. Paul regarded himself as (a) the chief apostle, (b) less than the least of all saints, (c) the first missionary.

6. The family of God is located at present (a) on earth, (b) in heaven, (c) both on earth and in heaven.

7. Christians are told by Paul to be rooted and grounded in (a) faith, (b) hope, (c) love.

8. We are to know, in all its dimensions, Christ's (a) love, (b) power, (c) glory.

9. When people get saved, the angels (a) rejoice, (b) intercede for them, (c) ignore the event.

10. The power available to the Christian is (a) only available to some, (b) imparted by the Holy Spirit, (c) very limited.

Turn to page 64 and check your answers.

The Unity of the Church

4:1-16

The doctrinal section of the epistle is now closed. The key note thus far has been "the hope of His calling" (1:18). To this point the book has dealt with the believer's exalted position—chosen, predestinated, sealed, called, quickened, risen, seated, coming again with Christ.

1. What is the key thought of the practical section of the epistle?

4:1 _____

The Bible's method of teaching is referred to by this verse. Everyday duties are to be built only on the strong foundation of the doctrine of Christ (I CORINTHIANS 3:11).

Chapter Outline

Unities of Grace	1-7
Diversities in Gifts	8-13
Essentials in Growth	14-16
Consequences of Growth	17-32

2. What word connects the thoughts of (1) our practice of Christianity and (2) our position in Christ?

4:1 _____

3. How will the realization of the loftiness of our calling immediately manifest itself in the life?

4:2 _____

4. What attitude is a person apt to have if he knows the lowly Jesus?

MATTHEW 11:29 _____

5. What is the first beatitude?

MATTHEW 5:3 _____

6. What is the element in which these qualities of character must function?

4:2 (last two words) _____

7. How does one get this love?

ROMANS 5:5 _____

8. State one of the primary duties of every Christian.

4:3 _____

_____

The word for "endeavor" means to "be diligent."

The basis for unity

9. Who is the author of unity?

4:3 _____

10. For what kind of unity did our Lord pray?

JOHN 17:21, 23 _____

This is no mere outward religious uniformity such as some men seek to bring about. The unity of the Spirit cannot be based on combinations and compromises. The Holy Spirit brings yielded believers into a spirit of fellowship regardless of minor differences. They are made to feel the throbbing of the same divine life. They love the same Lord because they are born of the same Spirit.

11. What is the doctrinal basis for this unity of the Spirit?

4:4-6 _____

_____

Here are certain fundamentals which form the basis of Christian fellowship: (1) The Church of Christ as a world-wide organism, not one religious sect. (2) One Spirit, Agent of regeneration, the power that holds true believers together. (3) One hope, salvation in Christ (COLOSSIANS 1:5), culminating in "the blessed hope" (TITUS 2:13). (4) One Lord to be worshiped (ROMANS 10:9). (5) One faith— Christ crucified, risen, ascended, coming again. (6) One baptism— the ordinance commanded by Christ as the gateway to the *visible* church (MATTHEW 28:19, 20). The reference here is probably not to the baptism of the Spirit, since the Spirit has already been mentioned in verse 4 (compare I CORINTHIANS 12:13).

12. When our Lord ascended to heaven, what two special signs of His deity were manifested?

4:8 _____

_____

13. When the spirit of Jesus departed at death and went into paradise, whom did He take with Him?

LUKE 23:43 _____

14. Where was the realm of departed spirits located at that time?

MATTHEW 12:40 _____

15. Prior to Christ's death upon the cross, what separated the spirits of the saved and the lost?

LUKE 16:25, 26 _____

16. Which direction did the spirit of Jesus go when it went into the paradise section of the realm of departed spirits (hades)?

4:9 _____

17. What did Christ do next after demonstrating to these saved spirits in paradise that His atoning sacrifice had at last been made?

4:10 _____

18. When Christ ascended, whom did He lead?

4:8 _____

19. What happened in Jerusalem when the spirit of Jesus returned and took up His body?

MATTHEW 27:52, 53 _____

_____

20. After Christ's resurrection, where did Paul say that paradise was located? (Give the direction.)

II CORINTHIANS 12:2-4 _____

21. Where would it appear that paradise is now located?

II CORINTHIANS 12:2 _____

22. At the time of His ascension Jesus gave evidence that the spirits in paradise (below) were being released to go above with Him. What other sign did He give?

4:8 _____

Spiritual gifts

23. What has the Holy Spirit been doing ever since for believers?

I CORINTHIANS 12:4-7 _____

_____

24. The Holy Spirit gives enablement to believers to make them effective servants. What were Christ's gifts to His Church?

4:11 _____

_____

25. Describe the nature of the work assigned to these persons.

4:12 _____

Some translate the words "for the perfecting of the saints" as "with a view to fitting His people for the work of the ministry for the building up of the body of Christ."

26. What is the purpose of the gospel in this age?

ACTS 15:14 _____

_____

The Body of Christ looks to the completion of this purpose. The purpose of the gospel ministry is to bring in the last one of the elect number so that Christ may return to receive His Church. Today some are trying to devise a completely new program for the church.

Unity through Christian maturity

27. When we begin to become "full grown" in Christ (verse 13), what will we supposedly leave behind?

4:14 _____

_____

_____

28. Describe the instability of the immature Christian.

4:14 _____

29. What kind of men and women are responsible for cults that entice people away from the true teachings of the Bible?

4:14 _____

_____

30. What happens to those who are in love with the truth of God's Word?

4:15 _____

31. How can a person effectively contend for the truth?

4:15 _____

Dr. Joseph Parker used to say: "Truth sits not on a throne bristling with bayonets, but on one established on the immovable basis of righteousness and infinite love." The formation of the Church is represented by an architectural metaphor in EPHESIANS 2:21, but in 4:16 the apostle borrows a physiological metaphor, illustrating from the growth of the human body.

32. If the body is to develop properly, what must every part contribute?

4:16 _____

As the members of the human body assist one another to health and maturity by working together, so must there be mutual helpfulness in the Body of Christ for spiritual growth.

check-up time No. 5

You have just studied some important truths about the unity of the Church. Review your study by re-reading the questions and your written answers. If you are not sure of an answer, reread the Scripture portion given to find the answer. Then take this test to see how well you understand important truths you have studied.

In the right-hand margin write "True" or "False" after each of the following statements.

1. God expects Christians to be meek and lowly. _____

2. Peace between Christians can be maintained without effort. _____

3. The true Author of Christian unity is the Holy Spirit. _____

4. The Lord's ascension was followed by His giving of gifts to men. _____

5. At His ascension, the Lord took others with Him to glory. _____

6. Paradise appears to be located, for the time being, in the underparts of the earth. _____

7. Christ's gifts to His church are men of spiritual enablement. _____

8. Spiritual gifts are given to believers so that they might bring glory to themselves. _____

9. Being swayed by one teaching, then another, shows spiritual immaturity. _____

10. Speaking the truth in love is really impossible. _____

Turn to page 64 and check your answers.

The Standard of
the Church

4:17—5:21

We come now to the more general exhortations. Note the "therefore" of verse 17, in view of the exalted positions just revealed.

1. In what should a Christian differ from people of the world?

4:17 _____

The word for "vanity" (empty) is one that indicates a waste of rational powers on wrong objects.

2. What is naturally expected of unregenerated people?

4:18 _____

By their spiritual ignorance, they are alienated from the life of God and have an aversion to the manner of life God requires. Harold Bell Wright once said: "I would rather receive a great vital truth from an illiterate backwoodsman who violates every rule of grammar, than have a university professor lie to me in perfect English."

3. When people have no capacity for moral or spiritual feeling, to what do they usually give themselves?

4:19 _____

4. When people "give themselves over" to lasciviousness (unbridled lust), what does God sometimes do?

ROMANS 1:24 _____

The words "uncleanness with greediness" mean a reckless delight in the things of the flesh.

5. What more can a believer do than "learn of Christ"?

4:20; compare MATTHEW 11:29 _____

_____

Many people learn certain ethical principles and moral ideas from Christ, but the Christian can take in Christ HIMSELF—His very character.

6. What is the word of the heavenly Father to all who seek truth?

MATTHEW 17:5 _____

7. State what Jesus said about truth being in Him.

JOHN 14:6 _____

Some today teach that believers should get their teachings only from the church epistles, not from Jesus.

8. Why is it essential for Christians to be taught the very words of Jesus?

JOHN 6:63 _____

9. What is the teaching of Paul regarding this?

COLOSSIANS 3:16 _____

10. Who is the wise man of today?

MATTHEW 7:24 _____

11. How is the "old man" (the Adamic nature) characterized?

4:22 _____

12. What should we reckon on regarding this old man?

ROMANS 6:6 _____

The new life

13. Describe the new change in the Christian.

4:23 _____

14. What are we to put on like an article of clothing?

ROMANS 13:14 _____

15. Name a serious sin in the life of some Christians.

4:25 _____

16. What should a Christian always be careful to do?

4:25 _____

If we owe truth to Christ, the Head of the Body, we also owe it to the fellow members of the same body. Would it not be absurd for one member of a human body to try to deceive another member?

17. When did Jesus manifest anger?

MARK 3:5 _____

Bishop Moule says: "Anger as a mere expression of wounded personality is sinful, for it means that self is in command. As a pure expression of repugnance to wrong, in loyalty to God, it is sinless where there is true occasion for it."

18. Even righteous indignation should not be nursed beyond what time of the day?

4:26 _____

42

19. If the devil gains control of us, where does the fault lie?

4:27 _____

20. If we have need of anything, how are we supposed to get it?

4:28 _____

Dr. R. A. Torrey said: "Stealing is taking anything from another without giving a just equivalent." Overcharging, underpaying, skimping in work could be so classified.

21. What should never pass the lips of a Christian?

4:29 _____

The translators were very polite. The Greek word really means "rotten talk." It is the same word that is used of decayed fish in MATTHEW 13:48.

22. Describe the only kind of talk that is supposed to come from the lips of Christians.

4:29 _____

23. List other characteristics that should not be found in Christians.

4:31 _____

_____

If we are without expressions of kind, humble and courteous behavior, how can unsaved people be expected to know that we are Christians?

24. When occasions of difference occur between us as Christians, what should we ever remember?

4:32 _____

25. When Christians are without the qualities that are the marks of a Christian, what is the effect on the Holy Spirit who abides within?

4:30 _____

26. Although we have often grieved the Holy Spirit, what can we say about His ministry toward us?

4:30; compare 1:13, 14 _____

_____

27. If one is truly born of the Spirit, unto what time is his salvation secure?

4:30 _____

A call to holy living

28. What is the startling exhortation of chapter 5?

5:1 _____

In verse 1 the Greek word for "followers" means "mimics."

29. In what special respect is the believer expected to show conformity of life with that of God?

5:2 _____

30. What is the badge of every true Christian?

JOHN 13:35 _____

31. Who are believers expected to mimic in these characteristics?

I PETER 2:19-23 _____

32. Restate Christ's special command.

JOHN 15:12 _____

33. List three sins that are not to be named among Christians.

5:3 _____

34. List other things which a Christian should not do.

5:4 _____

The word for "filthiness" means "baseness, obscenity."
The word for "foolish talking" means "fool talk."

35. What do fools always do?

PROVERBS 14:9 _____

36. At what point should every Christian always be on his guard?

TITUS 2:8 _____

Watch out for the chronic wisecrackers. They often keep on the fringe of the suggestive.

37. Who can definitely be considered as outside the kingdom of Christ?

5:5 _____

_____

Living in the light

38. What is said of those who are born again?

5:8 _____

The meaning here is that an unsaved person is one in whom the darkness of this world becomes visible. A true Christian is himself a light, because he has in him the Lord, who is "the light of the world."

39. With what is the fruit of the Spirit contrasted?

5:9; compare verse 11 _____

40. Describe the action of the Christian if he is to have influence against evil.

5:11 _____

41. What happens when one who is walking in the light is among sinful men?

5:13 _____

To the extent that we fellowship with those who are living to the flesh, laughing at their shady talk and apparently approving of their sinful acts, we are in danger of acting as they do before we know it. But a life that manifests the light of Christ penetrates the darkness of this world and brings conviction to the sinful.

42. If men want their lives to count against the darkness of this world, what must they do?

5:14 _____

Verse 14 is literally, "Stand up out of the dead ones and Christ shall shine upon thee."

43. Who are the dead ones?

EPHESIANS 2:1 _____

Responsibilities of Christians

44. Why is it sinful for Christians to fool away their time?

5:16 _____

The Greek for "redeeming the time" means literally, "buying up the opportunities"—a metaphor from traders who make the most of special seasons to move certain merchandise. The Christian should daily study to be an expert dealer in the commodities of time and opportunity.

45. What should take up all the Christian's time?

5:17 _____

46. In what way does Paul contrast the world's way of seeking hilarious happiness and the Christian's way of realizing the joy of salvation?

5:18 _____

47. While drunken people often sing their worldly songs, what does the Holy Spirit cause believers to do?

5:19, 20 _____

We may take wine in this passage as an illustration of the stimulants used by the unregenerated to secure exhilaration—the things of the senses, produced from without. But there is an "inner wine" that fills the soul with songs of gladness, giving true energy for external service.

48. State the command of Paul given here.

5:18 _____

49. When will the Holy Spirit take over the believer's life?

ROMANS 12:1, 2 _____

50. What will always be an outstanding characteristic of those who are filled with the Spirit?

5:20 _____

Said Chrysostom: "Let us give thanks not merely for manifest blessings, but also for those that are not manifest, and for those we sometimes receive against our wills."

check-up time No. 6

You have just studied some important truths about the standards of the early church. Now take this test to see how well you understand important truths you have studied.

Circle the letter of the correct or most nearly correct answer.

1. Paul says that Christians should differ from people of the world in (a) dress, (b) diet, (c) behavior.

2. Unsaved people are naturally mentally (a) alert, (b) darkened to spiritual things, (c) cleverer than Christians.

3. God sometimes "gives up" unsaved people who (a) sin frequently, (b) abandon themselves to vice, (c) ignore His Word.

4. When a person is saved he (a) needs to go on learning of Christ, (b) needs to know no more, (c) has no more problems.

5. To describe what is to be done with the old nature, Paul uses the figure of (a) slavery, (b) clothing, (c) marriage.

6. The Christian is to (a) give place to the devil, (b) flee from the devil, (c) resist the devil.

7. It is possible for a true Christian to (a) blaspheme the Spirit, (b) grieve the Spirit, (c) reject the Spirit.

8. The sins of fornication, uncleanness and covetousness are (a) not all equally serious, (b) all to be absent from a Christian's life, (c) overlooked in Christians by God.

9. The "fruit of the Spirit" is contrasted with (a) the works of the flesh, (b) the ways of the world, (c) the wiles of the devil.

10. Christians are to redeem the time because (a) it is easily lost, (b) the days are evil, (c) time is short.

Turn to page 64 and check your answers.

The Conduct of the Church

5:22—6:9

The apostle now begins exhortations regarding the discharge of relative duties. Rule No. 1, Christians owe one another mutual submission as members of the saved body. This is found in verse 21. The same submission is required of husbands and wives.

1. Unto whose husbands are wives to be submissive?

5:22 _____

Some women are more subject to other people than to the wishes of their own husbands—and some "rule the roost."

2. Although the wife is to be subject to her husband in marriage, what is said about the equality with the man?

GALATIANS 3:28 _____

3. The wife is to submit to the husband as unto whom?

5:22 _____

4. To whom did God originally assign the governing place?

GENESIS 3:16 _____

5. The headship of the man in the family is patterned after that of Christ. In what sense is the husband the head of the woman?

5:23 _____

Said Chrysostom: "Wouldst thou that thy wife obey thee? Then have a care for her as Christ does for the Church." It is the business of a head to look out for the interests of the body. Christ is not a dictator and unreasonable taskmaster over His Church.

6. How is a husband to treat his wife?

5:25, 28 _____

7. In what sense only is the wife subject to the husband?

5:24 _____

It is assumed that the wife has a husband who is "in the Lord" (compare 6:1) and devoted to her highest interests. She is subject "in everything" to which his authority extends justly and consistently with duty to Christ, the real Head. When husbands demand what Christ forbids, then the Supreme Head must rule. Let the wife remember, on the other hand, that "she who holds the heart of her husband and controls the conduct of her children, governs the state. She does it directly, positively, gloriously."

8. What tremendous obligation is laid upon the husband?

5:25 _____

9. What does the Bible say about a man doing the dishes?

II KINGS 21:13 _____

John B. Anthony was heard to say over the radio: "My dear man, if you want domestic happiness, multiply tender expressions, continue in gracious, gentlemanly conduct, and don't forget the potency of a few flowers once in a while."

10. How far did Christ's love for His Church go?

5:25 _____

The Church's sanctification

11. What was He seeking to do for His Church?

5:26 _____

Having mentioned Christ's love for His Church, the apostle now enlarges upon it, assigning the reasons why Christ gave Himself for it: to sanctify it in this world (verse 26), and glorify it in the next (verse 27).

12. Why does the Church, as a body, need cleansing?

5:27 _____

13. What is the "water" that must be applied?

JOHN 7:38, 39 _____

14. Name another type of cleansing mentioned in this chapter.

5:26 _____

15. What kind of washing does every member of the Body of Christ need?

TITUS 3:5 _____

16. How is a man to love his wife?

5:28 _____

17. What are most men very careful to do regarding their physical bodies?

5:29 _____

18. What does this imply as to a man's actions toward his wife?

5:29 _____

Marital responsibilities

19. State what the original pattern of marriage suggested as to the closeness of marital bonds.

5:31; compare GENESIS 2:23, 24 _____

20. In speaking of the relationship of husband and wife, what other relationship did the apostles have in mind?

5:32 _____

21. Who joins with Christ in the worldwide call for men to come to Him?

REVELATION 22:17 _____

Note that the "bride" here can be none other than the Church, for she comes down out of heaven with Christ, whereas Israel is the earthly people with promises related to the millennial earth.

There is no clash in the symbolism as some have imagined. The Church as Christ's Body receives life from the Head. As His Bride she receives divine love from her Husband. As a temple of stone she is the habitation of the Spirit. As a spiritual kingdom made up of subjects she is called upon for obedience to the King of kings (MATTHEW 13:43; EPHESIANS 5:5).

The apostle continues directions concerning the everyday duties of the Christian—all certain indications of the depth of Christian character.

Domestic duties

22. What is one decree of God for the well-being of the family and society?

6:1 _____

23. In subservience to whom are parents to exert authority in the family?

6:1 _____

24. State the first commandment with a promise attached.

6:2 _____

25. What is the promise?

6:3 _____

26. List one of the signs of depravity in the home mentioned by Paul.

ROMANS 1:30 _____

27. What is foretold concerning the home as one of the signs of the general decay in the last times?

II TIMOTHY 3:2 _____

28. What is said about the equal authority that father and mother have toward their children?

6:2; compare PROVERBS 1:8; 23:22 _____

_____

29. What is the father's duty negatively?

6:4 _____

30. State the father's duty positively.

6:4 _____

The Greek for "provoke not" means "exasperate not."

31. Why shouldn't the father exasperate his children?

COLOSSIANS 3:21 _____

When a father fails to set a good example he has no right to expect model conduct from a child. A father who cannot control his own temper is not fit to control a child who has lost his. It has been said that the first essential of training a child is to have more sense than the child.

32. How is a father to bring up his child?

6:4 _____

33. What is involved in the work of admonition?

DEUTERONOMY 6:6, 7 _____

_____

Masters and men

34. How could even the duties of a slave be sanctified?

6:5 _____

A good translation of "fear and trembling in singleness of your heart" is "with conscientious solitude and without duplicity."

35. What did the apostle think about a Christian working hard just when the employer is looking?

6:6 _____

36. In what way can one give honest measure in one's work for another?

6:6 _____

37. What is the way to serve even the hardest employer with good will?

6:7 _____

"With good will doing service" has been translated: "having his interests at heart." Employers are paying for this.

38. Although the employer may seem unappreciative and may not adequately remunerate his help, what is the sure way for a Christian to lay up lasting treasure?

6:8 _____

39. Under what obligation does God put the employer?

6:9 _____

_____

40. What should every employer bear in mind?

6:9 _____

Some manuscripts have, "both your and their [the employees'] Master is in heaven." Both employer and employee are accountable to God.

You have just studied some important truths about the conduct of Christians. Review your study by re-reading the questions and your written answers. If you are not sure of an answer, reread the Scripture portion given to find the answer. Then take this test to see how well you understand important truths you have studied.

In the right-hand margin write "True" or "False" after each of the following statements.

1. The wife is to be head of the home. _____

2. The husband is to love his wife as Christ loved the Church. _____

3. The husband-wife relationship is intended to illustrate that which exists between Christ and His Church. _____

4. The Word of God has a cleansing effect upon believers. _____

5. Disobedient children are a credit to Christian parents. _____

6. Parents who over-correct their children are making a big mistake. _____

7. The Holy Spirit tells employees to give whole-hearted service to their employers. _____

8. Every Christian should regard all work he does as being a ministry for Christ. _____

9. Employers are free of obligations towards their employees. _____

10. Every person in a position of authority must remember that he is likewise under the authority of God. _____

Turn to page 64 and check your answers.

The Weapons of the Church

6:10-24

In EPHESIANS 6:10-12 Paul reveals the conflict the Christian must face as a result of unseen powers; yet all-sufficient resources for protection are easily available.

1. In facing evil powers, what must take the place of natural wisdom and courage?

6:10; compare PHILIPPIANS 4:13 _____

_____

Verse 10 may be rendered: "Be strengthened in the Lord, and in the energy of him, the strong."

2. What must every Christian have to be victorious?

6:11 _____

Paul lay in the prison at Rome, chained to a soldier. His thoughts and language were colored by what he saw. In the outfit of the Roman legionary, he saw in symbols the supernatural dress of the Christian (see ROMANS 13:12; I THESSALONIANS 5:8).

3. State the eminent peril of every believer.

6:12 _____

Conybeare renders this verse: "The adversaries with whom we wrestle are not flesh and blood, but they are principalities, the powers and the sovereigns of this present darkness, the spirits of evil in the heavens above us."

The Christian's armor

4. What kind of weapons must be used to deal with such forces?

II CORINTHIANS 10:4 _____

5. Who will provide this armor?

6:11 _____

6. In whose strength will such forces be defeated?

6:10, 11 _____

7. Why is a *whole* armor needed?

6:13 _____

_____

8. How does one get (literally, "take-up"—help yourself) this armor?

6:13 _____

9. What must be done in addition to "withstanding" in this "evil day"?

6:13 _____

Conybeare translates verse 13: "And having overthrown, to stand unshaken."

10. What word found in verses 11 and 13 indicates that this is no concealed warfare, or "trench warfare"?

6:11, 13 _____

11. Name two parts of the armor that are given.

6:14 _____

12. What makes one morally firm against sin?

6:14 _____

13. Of what value is a knowledge of God's truth?

I PETER 1:13 _____

14. What relationship is there between the girdle and Christ?

6:14; JOHN 14: 6 _____

_____

15. If one is girded with truth, how does he manifest his vigor?

ROMANS 1:16 _____

16. Of what is the Christian's breastplate made?

6:14 _____

17. The heart protection provided by the Christian's breastplate comes from what kind of righteousness?

PHILIPPIANS 3:8-10 _____

18. What makes one's own righteous zeal ineffective?

ROMANS 10:2, 3 _____

19. State what one can say who wears this impenetrable armor.

ROMANS 8:33 _____

_____

20. What does the Christian need to give him firm spiritual footing?

6:15 _____

21. Describe the "gospel of peace."

COLOSSIANS 1:20 _____

_____

22. How can one be sure of his own standing before God?

ROMANS 5:1 _____

_____

23. What does the shield represent?

6:16 _____

24. When one has faith in the Word of God, how does he move forward?

HEBREWS 11:6 _____

25. By faith, what is he able to do?

6:16 _____

26. How did Jesus beat off the devil's attacks?

MATTHEW 4:4, 7, 10 _____

27. Describe the best head protection.

6:17 _____

28. What does the experience of salvation carry with it?

I JOHN 5:10 _____

29. Which is the great offensive weapon?

6:17 _____

30. Why does one who uses it get results?

HEBREWS 4:12 _____

_____

31. Why does use of this sword get eternal results?

ROMANS 10:17; I PETER 1:23-25 _____

_____

A closing prayer

32. What is all-important?

6:18 _____

33. Describe the kind of praying that never misses the mark.

6:18; compare ROMANS 8:26; JUDE 20 _____

_____

34. At what special time may this praying be directed to the throne of God?

6:18 _____

We say that the sails of a ship will carry it into harbor, and prayer may be called the sail that carries our heart's desires up to God. But wait! The sails alone cannot speed a vessel unless they are filled with a favorable breeze. The Holy Spirit must prompt the prayer and breathe God's desire through us, or our prayers will be like sails without a breeze—lifeless and useless. It takes Spirit-taught prayer to offset spiritual forces. No mere form of words will suffice.

check-up time No. 8

You have just studied some important truths about the weapons of the Church. Review your study by rereading the questions and your written answers. If you are not sure of an answer, reread the Scripture portion given to find the answer. Then take this test to see how well you understand important truths you have studied.

Circle the letter of the correct or most nearly correct answer.

1. The chief thing necessary in fighting our spiritual foes is (a) courage, (b) caution, (c) confidence in Christ.

2. Which of the following is *not* a part of the Christian's armor? (a) the shield of faith, (b) the helmet of salvation, (c) the fiery darts of righteous indignation.

3. The Christian defeats his foes (a) in his own strength, (b) in the power of the Lord, (c) in unity with other Christians.

4. When the Christian has done all that is required of him in his warfare, he is still called upon to (a) stand, (b) struggle, (c) sing.

5. The armor which has to do with righteousness protects the believer's (a) head, (b) hand, (c) heart.

6. The shield of faith protects us from (a) the attractions of the world, (b) the evil desires of the flesh, (c) the suggestions of Satan.

7. The one weapon for offensive warfare given to the Christian is (a) public testimony, (b) God's Word, (c) church fellowship.

8. We carry the attack into the enemy's strongholds when we (a) pray, (b) read our Bibles, (c) tithe.

9. A person girded with the truth will (a) boldly witness for Christ, (b) sometimes fall into error, (c) be able to dispense with the rest of his armor.

10. The Lord beat off Satan's attacks with (a) the shield of faith, (b) the sword of the Spirit, (c) the helmet of salvation.

Turn to page 64 and check your answers.

Suggestions for class use

1. The class teacher may wish to tear this page from each workbook as the answer key is on the reverse side.

2. The teacher should study the lesson first, filling in the blanks in the workbook. He should be prepared to give help to the class on some of the harder places in the lesson. He should also take the self-check tests himself, check his answers with the answer key and look up any question answered incorrectly.

3. Class sessions can be supplemented by the teacher's giving a talk or leading a discussion on the subject to be studied. The class could then fill in the workbook together as a group, in teams, or individually. If so desired by the teacher, however, this could be done at home. The self-check tests can be done as homework by the class.

4. The self-check tests can be corrected at the beginning of each class session. A brief discussion of the answers can serve as review for the previous lesson.

5. The teacher should motivate and encourage his students. Some public recognition might well be given to class members who successfully complete this course.

answer key

to self-check tests

Be sure to look up any questions you answered incorrectly.

Q gives the number of the test *question.*

A gives the correct *answer.*

R *refers* you to the place in the text where the correct answer is to be found.

Mark your wrong answers with an "x."

TEST 1			TEST 2			TEST 3			TEST 4		
Q	A	R	Q	A	R	Q	A	R	Q	A	R
1	F	3	1	a	1	1	T	1	1	a	1
2	T	7	2	b	2	2	T	4	2	c	10
3	T	6	3	c	5	3	F	8	3	b	14
4	T	14	4	c	10	4	T	10	4	c	17
5	F	17	5	a	11	5	F	11	5	b	22
6	F	22	6	c	11	6	T	21	6	c	29
7	T	24	7	c	12	7	T	24	7	c	32
8	F	26	8	c	13	8	F	31	8	a	33
9	T	28	9	b	14	9	T	33	9	a	27
10	T	21	10	a	12	10	T	45	10	b	30

TEST 5			TEST 6			TEST 7			TEST 8		
Q	A	R	Q	A	R	Q	A	R	Q	A	R
1	T	5	1	c	1	1	F	1	1	c	1
2	F	8	2	b	2	2	T	8	2	c	11
3	T	9	3	b	4	3	T	19	3	b	6
4	T	12	4	a	5	4	T	15	4	a	9
5	T	18	5	b	14	5	F	22	5	c	17
6	F	21	6	c	19	6	T	30	6	c	25
7	T	24	7	b	26	7	T	35	7	b	29
8	F	25	8	b	33	8	T	37	8	a	32
9	T	28	9	a	39	9	F	39	9	a	15
10	F	31	10	b	44	10	T	40	10	b	26

How well did you do?

0-1 wrong answers on any one test—excellent work

2-3 wrong answers on any one test—review these items carefully

4 or more wrong answers—restudy the lesson before going on to the next one